FORGOTTEN NECESSITIES

FORGOTTEN NECESSITIES

poems by

Jared Singer

Button Publishing Inc.
Minneapolis
2025

FORGOTTEN NECESSITIES
POETRY
AUTHOR: Jared Singer
EDITED BY: Tiffany Woodley
COVER DESIGN: Coral Black

◇

◇

button poetry

Published by Button Poetry
Minneapolis, MN 55418 | http://www.buttonpoetry.com

◇

Manufactured in the United States of America
PRINT ISBN: 978-1-63834-122-2
EBOOK ISBN: 978-1-63834-125-3

First printing

CONTENTS

FORGOTTEN NECESSITIES

Grief is like the rising sun,
inevitable and disorienting.
Without it nothing can grow.

SNOW AT DUSK

I hear the thunder of true silence
when the snow eats even echoes,
my own blood providing the drum I walk to.
I smell the memory of the city:
trash, weed, urine, and island cooking.
Echoes of the everyday.
It reminds me of the good kind of alone,
sitting by yourself on a mountain
before anyone you love has died.
I feel like anything is possible,
like each step is the beginning of a new life,
small and understandable.
I want to burn it all down.
I want to patch my boots.
I want to live somewhere else.

I AM COMFORTABLE FATTING OUT OF CLOTHING;

I hate myself a little more every time but
it's happened enough that it's a comfortable pain.

Like living with an old scar, or the prick of the needle
at the dentist's office. Like visiting a grave. Everyday pain.

Finding my clothes are loose enough to fall off
no matter how tight the belt, that any attempt to
wear suspenders ends up a three stooges routine
is a brand-new kind of terror. Like finding ice cubes
made of blood in a brunch mimosa.

I have worked hard for this; I know that it was,
and still is, the goal but I can't shake
the fact that part of me is missing.
I am less than I was a year ago,
less than I was yesterday.

I know I am burning fat, but I can't help but worry what else
I may lose with it. That fat was a lifelong companion.

What if I forget my favorite song, my favorite prayer? What if I forget
what my grandfather smelled like? What if I forget when my friends
died? What if I forget the burn of good whiskey and fresh
embarrassment? What if I forget my grandmother? My wife?

What if I wake up one day and I am a totally different, thin man?
Will fat me be remembered? Will anyone miss who I was? Will I?

MY BIRTH WAS A FLAWED BLESSING

I was given up for adoption immediately
by a woman who told the agency she never wanted
to be contacted about or by me.

The only information I have about my birth mother
is that I am not the first child she gave up.

That's the thing about blessings, about being human,
even though I was unwanted by her, I was still the answer
to someone's prayer; I was still a miracle.

I was still a wish my family had, that they thought
would never come true.

MOURNING ROUTINE 5

When the season of grief comes, put on your
mourning skin; knot your tie just a little too tight,
just noose enough to remember this is death's time.

Put on your sharpest cufflinks, let them bite into your wrists.
The pain will help you hold the tears in check or
let them rage, whichever is appropriate.

Put on your funereal shoes, the ones you haven't worn
since the last time you shoveled dirt on the lost.
The squared off ones that are dressy but matte, no shine today.

If you've gained weight, then slice the stitching just at the heel,
it will give enough for you to force your feet in. If you
have lost weight, then stuff the edges with handkerchiefs,

it will let you walk with dignity, and if you must give yours
to a stranger, you will still have a backup.
No one will say anything,
but if you show up to the burial
with brand new clothes, they will all notice.

From an outsider's distance the funeral looks like a sleepy wedding,
everyone looking their best but moving awfully slowly,
a stagger that could easily be the drunken end of the party.

It is only up close that the difference becomes skeletally sharp,
the strained smiles, the smart creases of the men's clothing,
the bleeding patterns of the women's.

When we gather to mourn, we are not a crowd, we are not
just a family, we are not friends or coworkers, we are a
collective, a beast with many mouths but no hunger.

Together we are simply an elegy.

MAP OF LONGING 1

Tonight, I watch the Caverns of Longing,
the places where we have been cut out of ourselves.

Hanging in the dark of your throat,
where once your uvula hung,
lies the Colony of Regret.
All the kind things
you never said huddle together,
trembling over the endless pit
that is your throat, tolling your failure
every time you open your mouth,
reminding you what that damned tongue is for.
Kindness can only thrive when shared.

The Colony of Regret is a starving hive,
where the kindnesses
you kept to yourself are too weak from hunger
to keep the town clean.

Each one that starves
keeps the village fed
for another day.

The only brightness in the Colony of Regret
is a single perfectly maintained shrine to hope.
The kindnesses scrub it clean with the clothes
off their backs, with their own hair when
they run out, mumbling prayers that
they are the last of their people.

TOOTH FAIRY

I wish I had kept my baby teeth in a jar,
instead of sliding them under my pillow
for the tooth fairy. 5 dollars apiece is
what I traded my bones for. I was eager
to do it. There is nothing I wouldn't
have traded for candy and trading cards.

I wouldn't wait for them to
wiggle their way out; I'd tie a string
between my tooth and the door
at the first sign of movement and slam
them out.

I wish I had them all now; I could rattle
them in that little jar, maybe scare away
aging for a little longer.

I'm not mad I sold my youth, just
that I sold it so cheap.

AN OPEN LETTER TO MISSED OPPORTUNITIES—

Dear don't knock my parents are home,
just climb in the basement window:

Dear third mixtape this month,
isn't there something so romantic about power ballads?:

Dear can we share a blanket every single
time everyone else goes to bed:

Dear breathy hey, turn the music up,
my mom is folding laundry:

Dear every whisper is close enough
your tongue brushes my ear:

Dear skinny dipping, on the day after Rosh Hashanah,
you yell happy new year as your leap into the river:

Dear purple bra under translucent white shirt the day
after I tell you my favorite color is purple,
I couldn't look away, and you couldn't stop laughing.
Even during the lecture about the rise of the Third Reich:

Dear licking the barbeque sauce off my gearshift, I don't even
remember the dirty joke you made, just that the words
automatic and hard were definitely said,
the only things I heard over my heartbeat:

Dear symphony of innuendo—
You are all cello bow pulled across no string.
The potential calamity of the bass drum
slammed with all the confidence of someone
who knows their lack of timing will be heard.
You are an entire orchestra of could have been.

You, all of you, rented a billboard on top of mount hormone
and screamed your **hints** until you were hoarse,
you wanted me to be tongue, and hand, and future.

But I was only howl.

So certain I was already carrion that instead of noticing
the affection I wanted with all the single-minded
ferocity of starvation; I spent my days playing
connect the dots with my scars,
turning the islands of broken that scatter my body
into an entire map of imagined worthlessness.

Potential can be hammer or anvil.
My greatest regret is that I let the ring
and peal of trying to find something,
anything to live for drown out the
many songs of joy you wanted to sing with me.

You were the air band;
I was the microphone,
if I had only known how close we were.

IS EVERYTHING OKAY

If you ask me again, I will lie.
I will pull out my own teeth in frustration.
I'll make you a necklace out of my molars
that you will have to wear around your neck,
forever.

Because of you I will never eat solid food again.
Next time you see me, I'll be gumming
Jell-O and other soft things ground from
the unspeakable parts of hard animals.
It will be your fault.

If you ask me again,
I will tell the truth
and that will be much,
much worse.

THE FUNCTIONING FAMILY EXAM (VERSION FOR THOSE WHO HAVE BEEN ADOPTED) PLEASE WRITE ALL ANSWERS IN PENCIL. YOU WILL CHANGE THEM LATER.

1) Families are
    a. Found
    b. Born
    c. Made

2) Name three people you would call on your death bed (include names and when they last let you down)

    ____
    ____
    ____
    ____
    ____
    ____

3) I found out I was adopted
    a. Before I can remember, I have always known
    b. When I discovered it on my own
    c. When my sibling used it as proof I was not loved
    d. In the court papers, during the divorce

4) I am loved
    a. True   b. False

5) Where are you from?

    ____
    ____

6) Where were you born? If the answer is the same as number five, then pause this test briefly to give a prayer of thanks or do a happy dance as your personal belief structure demands. If you do not know where you were born, then please answer only in metaphor.

____

____

____

7) Do you have any Brothers or Sisters?

a. Yes b. No c. Many

8) When you read number seven, did you assume the question was asking about

a. Birth siblings
b. Adopted siblings
c. Animals in a shelter
d. People you are not related to, but who would happily trade their breath for yours
e. All of the above

9) Do you want to find your parents?

a. I have my parents, I have no desire to find anyone who did not want me
b. Gd yes, whatever it takes
c. I don't need parents; my life is full as it is
d. What good have parents ever been

10) Imagine every kind thought someone thinks about you but never says stitches a single feather into your back, adding bone and muscle as needed. You are now an angel.

a. True b. False

HAUNTED

Those who are afraid of ghosts
have never been haunted by the living.
My mother still breathes,

but she flickers in and out of this world.
Sometimes she is as sharp as the kitchen
knife she loves so much.

Other times she is fuzzy around the edges.
Fuzzy like a memory, like the northern lights,
like satellite tv during a thunderstorm.

Sometimes my mother doesn't know how old I am
or what state I live in. Sometimes my mother says
her own name like a question.

My mother loves attention more than a puppy
in a room full of children
holding melting ice cream cones.

My mother is always in the room. Sometimes
she is so filled with questions and excitement it
is suffocating. Sometimes my mother is on the edge

of the room, silent, staring at nothing.
My mother is always alive, but not always alive.
Why would I fear a ghost when I can walk right through it?

FOREVER DECEMBER

There is still time to become a delicate thing.
There is no more time to ignore your father.
There is still time to grow towards the sun.
There is no more time to rage.
There is still time to flower, to seed.
There is no more time to be right.
There is still time to feed the honeybees.
There is no more time for silence.
There is still time to let go.
There is no more time to heal, he is almost 80.
There is still time to become something new.
There is just no more time. You've used it all.
There is still time for a miracle.
There is still time to call.

HOW TO WRITE A POEM ABOUT SUICIDE

Specific is the best general. Instead
of saying how you were related to the dead,
say what died with them: I lost my morning laughter,
my love of letters, my belief that nothing is beyond saving.
Make sure not a single line is the same length. It is okay
if they are similar. No day after their suicide will feel the
same, but they will all feel painfully similar.

Once you start writing, do not move until you are done.
Don't even twitch. The urge to stretch,
the urge to change anything, will remind you of the day it happened.

Mention the research but never the statistics.
You want to sound like an authority, but the personal
is all that matters here. When you use a term from the
research, define it and then hammer it home with emotion.
Suicide clusters, once one person in a community kills
themselves, it becomes far more likely others will do the same.
Misery is the only thing in the universe
that travels faster than light. Her brother has
written three suicide notes. One day he will sign
one, leave it for someone to find.

No one will believe a word you say unless
you include your relationship to suicide.
Talk about it like an old lover to a new flame;
don't name what you had, describe it in metaphor.

Only tell the truth. Use as many personal details as you can
stomach. Did you try it? How many times? Did you mean it
or did you just want someone else to notice? Was your relationship
with self-inflicted death even something that had a name?

I never tried to kill myself,
couldn't bear doing this to anyone else,
but I did
want to die,
for a long long time.

Don't type this poem, write it on the most durable paper
you can find. Whenever you get stuck, or start to cry,
crumple the damn thing like it was the note you found
or wished you'd seen. Take it all out
on the last words of your loved one because
they aren't around for you to take it out on them.
And you can't take it out on yourself. *See again,*
suicide clusters.

When you are done, sign the poem,
make sure to give yourself a moniker,
a title that you promise to earn in the future,
empathize. Rage. Be different.

Jared Singer, Survivor

23ANDME

I am adopted.
I am Jewish.
My mother gave me
a 23andMe kit
for Christmas.
A holiday I do not celebrate.

Never has a gift,
beautifully wrapped,
felt more like an obituary,
an eviction from
the only family that
chose me.

MOURNING ROUTINE 55

Do not haunt yourself.
Be careful with photos of the dead,
they are dangerous. Do not hide them.
Forgetting is a crime the dead will not tolerate.

Do not let them become shrines.
Do not make them the center of your
life. Our memories of the dead
can give us purpose. But if we let
lifeless images of our dead loved ones
overshadow our lives, we die twice.
I have met hundreds of ghosts, and
every single one had a pulse.

Put the photos in a drawer you open often,
or on a shelf you see regularly
out of the corner of your eye. Let your dead
haunt you occasionally, pleasantly, passingly.
Let their smile surprise you when you
need a pen to sign a letter, remember how gently
they held your hand when
you are dusting the shelves.

They are dead.
They don't have to be gone.
You are alive.
Act like it.

MAP OF LONGING 2

Tonight, I visit the Caverns of Longing,
the places where our empty should lie.

Floating on the acid sea, in the exact center
of your stomach, the one place in your body
where no flesh can be seen,
there is a small bubble city.

Here is where your excitement
for life's great firsts lived— First Kiss,
First Gasp, First Night Together.

Once, before shame flooded the place,
the inhabitants survived by raising great
flocks of iridescent butterflies— each one
a glory so grand that merely touching it would
leave you full and renewed. Not just healed—
having your hurts entirely unmade.

Now they survive by hunting the deep joys that
sometimes rise from the sea. They are all that's left.
There are fewer to catch every season.

The irony of surviving by slaughtering wild
laughter is not lost on those who sail these seas.

CLEAN

In the movies, when the hero
has to wash off blood, the
water never makes them clean:
it just spreads the blood like oil.
The only way for them to become
pure again is to scrub themselves
red raw with whatever wash cloth,
sponge, or other easily stainable
object is close at hand. It makes
for a beautiful metaphor.

In my experience, blood washes off
remarkably clean. No soap scum
or slickness lingers on your body—
just filthy one moment and then clean
the next. The water doesn't turn pink,
doesn't froth; there's no poetic image of transition.

Just clear before it hits you and red when it
plummets to the drain. Dark or bright,
depending where the blood came from.
Here is what they don't tell you,

the blood looks the same
whether it comes from you,
the chicken, or the man who
forced you to swing on him
like you have wanted to
swing on yourself
for so many years.

BONE AND INK

I can admit it now;
I loved when they hit me.

Not because I liked the pain
or believed I deserved it but because
it was the only time I was
allowed to be what they called me.

Animal. When you are surrounded,
when they will not leave your dignity,
when they do not believe you are human—
remind them.

Before all of this there was bone
and fist and teeth. I didn't win
too many fights, but they bled

and broke as much as I did.
I read in my favorite play, on one of the days I
was allowed to be human, "you fool!
as if the way one falls down matters!"

"When the fall is all that's left, it
matters a great deal." They believed,
deep in the thorny parts of themselves,
that because I was adopted, I had no past,
and because I was Jewish, I deserved no future.

They forgot that it is the grind
and smash that gives
us ink. That we cannot read or write
if we are not willing to bleed for it. Berries make
the brightest hues, but bone will work when it must.
No one tells us this.

FAILED OPTIMISM

My father worries I'm a pessimist.
He tells me he wishes I'd try harder
to see the glass as half full,
that if we work together we can fill
the whole damn thing.

He believes we can fill every glass.

I tell him I never worry about how full
the glass is; it's irrelevant. I worry
that no matter what some selfish
(or even worse, careless) asshole
will just smash the glass on the ground.

I worry about a tongue shredded by glass
as I try to save what little I can.

My dad laughs, tells the story to his friends,
smiles at how clever I am, admires my ability
to turn a phrase.

My father still thinks I'm joking.

MOURNING ROUTINE 9

Your burdens belong to you, bend them to your will.
Everything is going to remind you of your lost one; it
is good to weep, but do not let it bury you. They'd hate that.
There is already one less light in this world,
do not let their loss make yours gutter out also.

Every time you imagine their reflection, wrap yourself
in the warmth of their memory. When you see their face
in the socks on your floor, say a favorite memory
for each one you gently place into the basket.

When someone on the subway makes a sarcastic comment,
then winks just like they used to, laugh all the way
from your toes. It doesn't matter if strangers think you crazy,
laugh every fucking chance you get. Then laugh
again, at the way you say fucking in your head just
like they used to say it aloud, hitch in the middle
and everything.

When you catch them out of the corner of your eye,
don't you dare get depressed because it turned out
to be a stranger with the same haircut, you take that
gift, that single moment where they seemed back in
your life, and say to the wind something you wish
you had said to them.

When it's too much, when coincidence piles upon tragedy,
when the whole world is grief and ghosts, when you can't
remember how to do the simplest things like check a bandage
or feed yourself because you are drowning in loss,
take a breath. Realize how lucky you are.
You are surrounded by someone you love.
Even though they are dead, they are still everywhere. Think
how much joy just one of them brought you. Now remember
you have dozens. Laugh, then laugh again. Even if you choke.

LEARNING

For Bill Hunley

There has always been something hollow in me,
something that can only be filled with more.
Every new experience is cotton candy—
satisfying only for the time it takes to consume it.

There is a man who taught me the names
of the trees that gave me shade,
which plants I could eat and what
turtles I could pick up without risking a finger.

He taught me how to catch crayfish.
Taught me the names of their body parts
while they struggled in his hands.

When done, he released them so gently,
the water remained crisp, silt-less, not even a ripple.

I knew this was magic. He called it science,
gave me a name for my first love.

The first time I tried to hunt my own crayfish
(silly, calling it hunting, wanting to imagine myself
fierce and final) the pincer slashed my finger.

Blood welling as I held the desperate, fragile beast.
This man warned me to be careful;
Knowledge will often make you bleed.

This is fine, blood teaches best.
But you must make sure that your
exploration hurts only you. Let the little thing go.

He gave me a name for my hollow. Curiosity.

TASKED BY LOVE

My wife says that my voice is the ultimate prize.
I don't know if this is the kindest thing she has
ever said to me or the cruelest joke.

By the look on her face, my wife doesn't know either,
but she hopes that it is gentle. She wants it to be kind.
We are watching our favorite show, where five
comedians humiliate themselves for fame and to satiate
an island nation's need for laughter, a hunger that grows
more desperate as their influence on the world wanes.

It always starts with the sacrifice, where each contestant
offers a prize to whet the comedy Gd's unending thirst.
Today's prize category is "nicest thing you can hold, but barely."

My wife offers up my voice, says it is because she knows
I can carry a tune, but only just. My wife smiles when I sing,
the same flavor of smile as when she sees a dead baby bird,
the one that holds back her tears, the one that says she
wishes the world were a better place.

My wife listens to my voice with the patience and kindness
of an old willow tree. She knows there is nothing in
the world I wish I could do more than sing, more
than lift up a room with just my voice. My wife
knows I would trade everything I am for this.
She smiles, knows she has offered up the best prize.

FIRST LOVE

In high school, I dated a woman who
wore a promise ring and a cross everywhere.
She rubbed her cross whenever she was nervous
or excited. It was once bright gold and carved
with the face of her lord.

By the time we kissed, it no longer shined,
its new color tarnish and sweat, the pad
of her thumb had rubbed away the details
of Jesus's face until it was just an empty mask.

The only time she ever took off her ring or her
necklace was when we were naked. She
wasn't willing to let even her now faceless
Gd see her with a jew, with me.

The first time this happened, I froze, said I wasn't
willing to be a broken oath or a hidden thing.
She said I was neither.

She said she wasn't the same person who
had made that promise. That she'd broken
it the year before anyway. She pulled my hands to her naked
body and, thick with want, said that it was okay
if love and faith never met in the middle.

I didn't know what a kiss was supposed to taste like,
didn't know how passion was supposed to move.
I only knew that she tasted of promises and lies, like too sweet
coffee, burnt. I know that when we were done I always
felt sweaty and tarnished, and sometimes, utterly faceless.

INSTRUCTIONS ON BEING BETTER

Monday, April 1st 2024 edition

Bleed, spit, breathe.
Hate yourself, laugh, laugh again.
Run, limp, crawl.
Solve a puzzle, ask for help, be proud.
Try, fail, win anyway. Bargain,
listen, really listen. Embrace joy, don't forget to express it,
choke.
Forgive, forgive, forgive, even yourself.
Be honest, hate
only the parts of yourself that do you no good.
The rage is something
you can love; it heals more often than not. Look at the dirt
caked under your nails,
know that you are clean. Do not plan everything. Trust,
hope,
rest.

MOURNING ROUTINE 27

Start every morning with a song,
one you have never sung before.
Sing it loud enough for heaven to hear,
loud enough for six feet of dirt and
three inches of pine.

Make it a song they loved, or one
they would have loved
had it been written before they died.
When you run out, and you will run out,
make up your own songs to melodies
they loved.

Never sing a dirge, make every song an anthem,
an ode, sing so hard it's like you hate breathing.
Songs about the dead are depressing. Songs
for the dead are undeniably joyous.
It could not matter less if you are on key,
only that you sing with abandon.

Do this day after day until there is no more
music left, until all the songbirds in your dreams
have collapsed from exhaustion, until the
soundtrack to your life has faded, until
it is indistinguishable from traffic. Until you are
a whole new kind of hollow.

On this blessed day, sit in the dark with a single candle
and celebrate a brand-new kind of birthday.
Know that now you can step past this loss. For even
hollow, you filled the world with songs for the dead.
You filled the space they left not with noise, but with
joyful exultation. Even broken, alone, and lost
you made something new. Something they
would have loved.

MAP OF LONGING 3

Tonight, I roam the Caverns of Longing,
those places where lonely exists
even when alone does not.

In the right eardrum there lives a single man.
His one room cottage has no kitchen,
there is just his moldy straw bed on one wall
and all the instruments he used to play on the other.
Once, twice, many times before, he played
the background music for all you loved,
you never knew he was there, but he was
always your favorite.

A day after the last time
you heard her say your name,
the day you found
out she died, was the last time
you let him play.

The roof of his cottage never stops leaking,
but he has nothing to patch it with except wax,
and if he took that, the world outside would be too loud,
too final for either of you to breathe.

MONOLOGUING

To be read while listening to Blink 182's "All the Small Things"

I love musicals.
Well okay, I love *The Nightmare Before Christmas*,
and *Moulin Rouge*, and *In The Heights.*
Well, I love the first 30 minutes,
when the songs are fast, loud
and full of desperate yearning.
There is little I love more than hearing
someone trying to sing a better world
into being.

Quiet longing makes my throat close.
Hope can live in the dark, the glow of purpose
slowly building until we are found. But silence can
strangle it between breaths, leaving us with nothing,
Not even potential.

My doctor told me that there is a
small chance I may lose the ability
to speak in a few years. This made me question

what I want to use my voice for in the time I may have left.
I find the "important things" of little interest,
talking about politics, ethics, climate change
all feel like a great waste of a good voice.
I can argue these things in an essay, or a book
when the time comes— Even with my middle finger
if necessary.

Telling my loved ones the obvious and important,
that they are the only things worth building a life on,
that their love is everything, seems silly. A well thought
out hand-written note will say this as well as I can.

I've decided the best use of my air is making my wife laugh
as loudly and often as possible.

Her laughter is a rainstorm on the hottest day,
one I never get tired of walking slowly through.
I need it, like breathing. I want to make her laugh
as long as I still have a voice,
still have comedic timing,
still have my tongue.

THALASSOPHOBIA

I can hear the deep calling my name. It bellows for me, loud enough
to drown the beaches, but so far down it's a lover's whisper, softly
promising to take the slow burn of bright on flesh away. I don't
want to die alone, and the ocean promises I won't. There are
infinite ways to die below the waves, and honest woman
that she is, the Ocean promises no gentle end. I'd suffer,
but I would not be alone; there is water everywhere. If I
drown, it will fill my empty places at last. If I sink, she
will hold me tight enough to make diamonds.
If her children take me, it will be a symphony
of perfect teeth, the shred of my flesh sharp
and clean. Imagine a world where no one
has a broken smile, where even bone is
replaceable. When a whale falls and its
corpse hits the ocean floor, it creates a
jungle that lasts for decades. The heat
of its body a blessing allowing life
where before none was possible.
Clouds of fish swarm, turning
every scrap into thriving life.
It would be the first time
my fat was a blessing.
Dead, but whole.
Irreplaceable.
Forgotten.
At peace.

STRIDE

My wife walks like it's her first day in this body,
like she's a cartoon foal at the beginning of a Disney movie,
like she never read the manual. She leads with her head and
her chest, so off-balance every step she takes is a miracle.
She never falls. My wife laughs at the laws of nature,
and at me.

When my wife laughs, it feels like gravity is reversed.
I damn near fly. Conservation of momentum means nothing to my
wife. When she forces her arms to stop swinging, there's still a
movement to them, like her shoulders are about to fly away.
My wife walks full throttle, even at a mosey her body
looks like it's sprinting. The way she walks defies physics.

My wife should star in battery commercials.
She always looks like she is trying to run through a tunnel
painted on a wall, like if she vibrates enough nothing can stop her.
My wife walks like she's going to live forever, like death is a cardboard
cutout she can Kool-Aid Man through. My wife is a perpetual motion
machine. My wife walks like she's going to die any second, and she
wants to squeeze the most out of every breath.
My wife walks like she's on her way to save us all, and there
has never been anything more worth saving. My wife walks
everywhere.

LATE AUGUST

Words in italics are taken from Emily Zogbi's "Ode to Crazy Girls"

The end is here

I slice enough carrots and cheese for thirty
people whose mouths are not already filled with grief.
I time the thunk of blade into cutting board
so it breaks up the silence of people who know
nothing they say will help. I am the first one to laugh,
it's faker than the smile causing my dimple to flair,
but it starts a slow cascade of laughter that blooms like the
flowers everyone brought and no one asked for.
No one ever says wake, or shiva, instead
everyone says the word party, like it's a spell
that will turn the eulogies into gleeful toasts.
When it's time for the well-wishers to return to their joy
and for the deepest mourners to be alone with their ghosts,
I clean, loudly and in the middle of conversations,
as if to say this house and our hearts are as empty
as these cups, and it is time to take them out.
Sometimes the only company that will do is our dead.

and the end is a good friend of mine

HEARTH FIRE

As I am about to go, you raise
your index finger, the most you've
moved all day, say *this story is worth*
a minute of your time before you go.

Any story you tell me is worth
as much time as it takes.

Not because you are dying,
though you are, but because
you are a good man
whose eyes light up when
I listen.

ACHILLES

Achilles's top web search is "foot fetish
show full leg." His browser history
would make Zeus blush.

The idea of someone's sweat-covered
foot near his mouth makes Achilles gag.
The image of licking someone's toes,
knowing just how many breeds of fungus
and bacteria grow under the nail
makes him vomit.

Still, he watches every scene; they are the only
thing that gets him hot. He bookmarks
every video he can find where someone licks an
ankle.

What no one tells you is that
someone who cannot be hurt
is always alone. The man who has
no weakness by definition has no love.
To fall in love is to be vulnerable.

Achilles was the loneliest man in the world
until he found Briseis, a woman who knew
the secret fact that there cannot be closeness
without pain.

She ignored his muscles, his mouth, all the
parts of his body others lusted for and instead
kissed his tendons.

He didn't know he could be loved like this,
didn't know he was worthy of someone
changing what they desired for him.

When you understand another's wants like that—
like mist made solid, suddenly a single tendon
is the most beautiful thing in the world.

When Briseis was torn from him,
he thought he would never love again
until Patroclus taught him that a man
could be that gentle too, that you
can find vulnerability in other men,
that you do not have to be
invincible. When they kissed,
Olympus shook.

When jealous Eris released the Apple of Discord into the
world, she meant it to shatter even the idea of peace.
It only worked on the Gds, humans were spared.

I believe Achilles and Patroclus are why.
Their kiss was the Apple's opposite.
Theirs was the kiss of peace.
The kiss of gentle.
This was human on human.
This was love, focused and pure.

Patroclus was murdered, and Achilles tried
to drown the world in blood.

Now he searches the internet for a pale
shadow of what he once had.
There is nothing sexier in this world than knowing
someone could hurt you but never would.

SIMPLE LOVE

When we first started dating, your snoring kept me up
every night; there were days I didn't stay over just so I could sleep.

Now, on the nights I have to sleep without you, I play movies filled with distant gunfire, muffled explosions, and heavy-duty construction just so I don't feel so alone. I cannot sleep without an echo of your snorts

MOURNING ROUTINE 37

Human beings are not meant to mourn alone.
Grief is a blanket of nails the size of an incoming storm;
it cannot be stopped, and you cannot get out of the way.

Try to bear it alone and all that makes you human will pour
out the gashes leaving you a ventriloquist doll made of meat—
hollow and only able to speak at another's command.

When you are loved by enough of the living, each of you
takes a piece of the blanket and holds it aloft, spreading
your palms flat against the nails, sharing the pressure.

You all bleed, you all suffer, and none of you look directly
at the grief. It, like an eclipse, will blind the foolish. You pass
it over your heads one bloody palm print at a time until

the sun passes from behind the grief, searingly bright,
uncomfortably warm, and utterly beautiful. None of you will laugh,
not yet, but your tongues will loosen and your scars will bond.

THE WORST BIRTHDAY EVER, A FACTUAL RETELLING.

I am standing in the kitchen
with two of my best friends,
the only person not standing in this
room who called me today is my sister.

We are drunk on the worst whiskey
I have ever had. I don't know how,
but we got on the subject
of everyone who should be here,
everyone who should have called.

The apartment feels full.
It is empty. We finish the bottle
with a final toast for the night,
a line from one of my favorite songs—
"All I ever wanted was to pick apart the day
Put the pieces back together my way."

A desire so simple that we knew it was impossible.

THE WORST BIRTHDAY EVER,
A STORY OF SLIGHT EXAGGERATION

My whole family is there,
crammed into my tiny Brooklyn
apartment. Everyone. Even the dead.

My grandmother, skin ten-years rotten,
is shooing everyone out of the kitchen,
this is a party and she is going to make
her butter cookies *dammit,* it's so much
easier now her arthritis is gone.

My dad has my nephew cornered
by the bathroom. My nephew is so newly
dead you can almost see his chest move.
If you didn't know, he'd look right at home
in freshman orientation. My father keeps
asking him questions about the accident.
Was he speeding? Drinking? Was it the other
driver's fault? My father's questions come
with the desperation of a failing prosecutor,
like if he gets an answer that he can make sense
of, it will bring him back.

My nephew awkwardly dodges his questions
while he eavesdrops on the other cousins talking
about college experiences he will never have.
He drinks in every detail like he's dying
a second time of thirst.

My bio parents walked through the room once,
stayed seven seconds, just long enough
to change the course of the whole party. They
were faceless, no defining features at all, just
medical histories stapled to their colorless shirts.
They flickered in and out, neither the living or the dead
able to tell which side of the bridge they stand on.

After they left, in the living room corner,
right in front of the speakers,
there appeared a cloud of potential blood siblings
chain smoking possibility. The whole apartment
reeks of it; I'll never be able to get it out
of the furniture. Every time I look over
at them, there is a different number.
One, three, seven, once there was a whole bus full.
They talk to nobody, just take turns glaring at me
and my adopted (read real) sister.

My stepfather is causing a scene.
I love this for him. He has parked the
wheelchair he used to need by the front door
to the apartment and is challenging everyone
who walks by him to a race from wherever they happen
to be to the wheelchair. He makes the loser sit in
the damn thing for an hour. He hasn't lost yet.
Whenever someone refuses to race
or tries to get out of the chair early,
he dances around them calling them spoil sports
and dirty breathing cheaters. My mom is watching
him silently from the couch, with a smile wide
enough to swallow grief.

I try to keep people out of my bedroom,
but it's just so crowded people keep sneaking in.
All of my exes are hiding under the bed, holding
hands and whispering at everyone who walks
by each of my many failings, both real and perceived.
I asked them what they were doing under there,
and my first love said they wanted to hide in the closet
for symbolism's sake, but it was packed. I said yeah,
all my dead friends are playing dungeons and dragons
in there. They wanted to come to the party to support me
but didn't want to drag the mood down or separate
me from the living. They did always love me better than
I deserved.

The clock is about to strike midnight,
my birthday is almost over. I rush to find enough
glasses so that everyone can share a toast. I end up
having to use every object in the house that can hold liquid,
the glasses, bowls, pots, even the shoes and hats.
We have just enough. As the clock chimes and the magic
unravels, we all repeat my favorite toast. No one's voice
is raised, but there are enough of us that it shakes the house.
"To us, and those like us, there are damn few left."

MAP OF LONGING 4

Tonight, I am lost in the Caverns of Longing.

Your fingertips have been hollowed out.
It's why they ache in the cold; it's why they
crack whenever you are nervous.

A hard people live there.
Once, there was nothing but an unfeeling
wall of bone at the ends of your hands, but
these stubborn bastards dug hard and true.

They hollowed out your fingers and have made
fortresses in your knuckles from which they ply
their trade. Every time you strike a key, or write
a word, or tap your knee, there is an earthquake
inside your hands.

The sensible people stay deep in the body, where
every fitful movement you make doesn't threaten
a cave-in, but the Knuckle People are made of stern
stuff and know that what they dig for is well worth
their lives.

They mine your fingertips for pride. Every time
you make something, another vein appears,
every time you hold your wife's hand
or tie your child's shoe. The problem is, every
time you do something you know, there is less bounty.
It's getting harder to harvest enough pride to feed them all;
in small gatherings, the great miners of the Knuckles speak
of what their children will do when there is nothing left.
Some tell legends of the spine, a mountain chain of
unending pride, but others know deep in their heart
that times are hard everywhere and that this body
is running dry. These meetings are full of curses
and prayers, of empty looks and brave bellows. Of
starving, beautiful hope.

CORPORATE THINKS SUICIDE IS FUNNY

Corporate thinks lynching is a cute anecdote
to tell your children around the dinner table.

In 2004, Best Buy gave everyone who bought
a geek squad service plan a "free" gift,
it was a USB cable that read

"In the event of a technological
catastrophe, do not use the USB
cable as a noose; instead
contact a geek squad agent
immediately."

Corporate is happy for you to choke,
happy for you to die slowly,
feet swinging, desperate,
as long as it raises brand awareness.

MY COUNTRY, EXPLAINED

I am 39 years old.
I am fat, out of shape,
and I have dragged myself past
a thousand miles of hard road.
I am also white.

Which means despite every hurt
I have put my body through,
there is a good chance I will outlive
my best friend even though he is healthy
and athletic.

This is because he is black
and too tall to hide in a crowd,
and has a good enough heart
that he is compelled to speak when
he knows something is wrong,
and he is eloquent enough
that others may listen.

This is what it means to be American.

cANCER

Whenever I talk about cancer,
I give it a name that's easy to sneer at,
a name that would make most parents
roll their eyes if it belonged to their child's
partner. anastasia, kayleigh, fabio, strider.
When I am feeling particularly petulant,
brantley.

When we name something, we are attempting
to give it purpose. The only purpose I am willing to give
cancer is to inspire derision.

I heard once, in a story I desperately want to believe,
of a child who thought we capitalized names as a sign
of respect, so for their whole childhood they refused
to capitalize the names of george bush, hitler, or their
step-father gary. Fuck gary.

And cancer.
cancer is the spoiled toddler
Death has to clean up after.

Let's laugh when we hear its name.

PARTICULARLY GIBBOUS

There is a young girl who controls the tides—
This is not a metaphor.
The moon is tucked under her tongue
like a pearl, beautiful and irritating.
She has tried to floss it out, but
her skin grows around the base.

She almost never speaks. When
she opens her mouth, the moon, angry
at its captivity, does everything the
legends claim it can. Tricks are played
on all who lack respect,
foolish wishes are granted,
and the tides wipe the arrogant away.

Because of her silence, her parents worry
she's not normal and have whispered conversations with
doctors they will never tell her about.
Adults often see acting responsibly
as deviant behavior.

She is becoming a phenomenal communicator.
She knows she can never say a single word in anger,
never lose control for a single syllable. An errant
whisper could turn her mother into a deer, grant
her brothers' wish for silence, or even drown
the whole damn tourist town.

She communicates with only gentle touches and shy smiles—
most ignore her, think her foolish, but those who notice
know she is sharing the best kind of secrets, those
that have been held by the moon since before
life first left the sea.

RISE

I have always thought we learned the wrong lesson
from Icarus. Who cares about the fall. Who cares
if our wings melt. Who cares if we smash our bodies
into the ground. Who cares if we die

broken. Our life is not defined by our last moment.
Having nothing left does not make us a failure.
We are defined entirely by how far we reach.

And Icarus, that beautiful, enviable, glorious failure,
reached for the sun. He sought light and enlightenment
with his whole being.

His father gave him a humble gift, said you can touch the sky,
but only for a moment; don't stray too far. Icarus responded—

I can touch the sky.
I will live there for the rest of my life.
I will kiss the moon.
I will ride the sun.

Icarus knew he'd rather die
than reach one inch less than he could.

Icarus knew that most important truth,
that we humans are explorers, that curiosity is more
important than life itself.

HEPHAESTUS

Gd of fire and forge,
the greatest artisan in history,
is a fraud. He is proud of this.

He lives by himself, in a workshop
carved deep within Mount Olympus.
He has a thousand tv's constantly
playing every gossip show, every
runway contest, every commercial
simultaneously. The sheer noise
would shatter a mortal's skull.

Hephaestus, who made all the greatest
marvels the world has seen— who forged
Zeus's thunderbolts, who made the chariot
that pulled the sun itself, whose work was so delicate
he made a man of bronze who could breathe—
now makes knockoffs

by the million. He doesn't even take credit for
them. Every single thing he crafts says "Made In
China", by his own estimate, he makes half the fakes
in the world.

Once, when the world was small, and the petty
antics of his family were the most important events
in it, Hephaestus inspired by crafting inimitable
masterworks. Now in a world of 8 billion, where more
people are born in a single week than populated
the planet when his family ruled, he has realized
a simple truth— humanity's greatest barrier
to creation is no longer a lack of inspiration, it
is greed. It is the sheer weight of 8 billion breathing
creatures trying to exist in a world where there will
never be enough resources. 8 billion human minds
can create what he never could— if they had a chance.
The best way he can help is selling 10 dollar shoes.

ORNAMENT

There is silver sown into her skin covering all
the places men covet and shame. *Your beauty*
must outshine the sun, they whisper, lust
and drool flooding out of their mouths, blinding
as fog. Flesh alone is enough

to make them croak, more toad than man. The mere
idea of covering that which they treasure
with treasure burns them whole. When they made
her more desire and less human, they forgot
that silver tarnishes, that it goes green

with time and air. She is tired of rubbing herself rough
for others. She has no good options. She loves her body
best when it glows, but that is when their fingers
slither and their eyes dig the most. Her hips and breasts
are always tarnished by their thieving paws. Shame

grows behind her eyes like grass in an untilled
field. They want her tiny enough to hang
on the wall with the other objects they own and
have forgotten. She sings of beauty buried, of

overgrown gardens no longer touched
by man. She sings of their mothers and sisters.
They do not try to understand.

POSSIBILITY

After Renee Gregorio's "Whatever Is"

Not the rip of the shuffle
but the bend of the cards

Not the tear of skin
but the well of blood

Not the prayer
but the language

Not the rabbi
but the unending peal of the shofar

Not the shame
but the laughter

Not the love
but the separation

Not the burial
but the dirt

Not the note
but the song

Not the breath
but the holding

Not what is
but what could be

Not our desire
but our potential

CHARON'S OBOL

When you walk the soul road,
you leave everything behind.
Your pains, all of them, finally

gone. That ache you've had
since you were nineteen when you broke
seven ribs, gone. The knee that called the rain,

gone. The scar, burned behind
your eyes when you realized she was
really dead, gone. The distended

place where your self-hate lived, always
glutted or malnourished, never once
adequate, gone. So too with your joys—

her laugh, gone. The gentle touch
tracing your scars, gone. The aching joy of
scaling the mountain, gone. All the first kisses,

gone. The trust, of a good dog,
more thorough than any you have managed, gone.
There is only one thing you get to take across the last river.

A single word, the one you love most. Make it your
own and hide it well. There is an ocean of lost souls
who never loved a single idea enough to hold onto

their human after death. They will try to steal yours.
I will carve the word 'echo' into my pinky finger.
I've broken it six times, enough that I could grape

it off the vine that is my hand easy enough.
A single pain, sudden and sweet. Echo, that
champion of joy and handmaiden of loss,

I will carve your truth into my bones.
Echo's essence— each moment is unique.
You can't repeat your greatest ecstasies

or your deepest failures, but you can learn
from them. Replay their echoes in your
heart a thousand times until you get them right.

You've endured, blood turned frozen snowflakes.
You cannot change your past, but you can learn.
Every shout into a ravine, a request to be taught,

a lesson only you know. Am I worthy?
am I worthy?
am   I   worthy?

I will hide the echo in a broken tooth, that
failed castle. Consumption, protection,
and weakness all in one.

My teeth are jagged and frail,
but they still snap and tear,
echoes of when I was strong.

Death will take my body,
my memory, my love,
but it cannot take the
reverberations

of what I have done. You'll
hear my snarl in every thunderpeal
long after I'm gone.

MOURNING ROUTINE 1

Don't forget to mourn yourself.
We have all lived many lives.

If someone you truly loved dies,
chances are one of your selves died with them.

Every relationship has its own language. They have died,
and now the language you shared with them is extinct.

Forget not the person you grieve but also
mourn the person you were around them,

who they made you want to be.
Who they made you know you could become.

Hold a wake for your lost self. Invite all the people
you used to be, all the you's that you've buried.

Tell stories about what made this you unique,
it's the only one that ever sprayed milk out its nose,

it is the one who hated themselves the least,
they were the fastest to trust.

Not only are you mourner, you are archeologist,
archivist, and phantom.

Remember what you've lost. Remember
how much of that same you still have.

RAGGED BREATH

I am a burst orange.
        I make the merchant weep,
unmarketable waste.
        Wet flesh exposed to air
is the easiest to consume,
        discarded but filling. Human.

WHEN I LET GO OF YOUR HAND

your fingers drag against the scars on my palm.
I hear your mother crying for
the grandchildren she won't have.

I taste her manicotti recipe for the last time.
The phantom sauce makes me drool.

I wonder if I will ever feel so attractive again.

I swear I can see your hands
bleed where my wounds were.

(IN MY WORST NIGHTMARES I AM) TOOTHLESS

Our teeth were made to hold our conscience.
This is why young children so often lack empathy—
they have yet to pull their ego out of their
mouth, bloody, and offer it up to a stranger as a gift.

Our consciences are strong enough to crack bone—
castles our bodies grew to guard that which is most
precious, but if we do not care for them, they will erode,
crack, and maybe even poison our blood.
This is something no one tells you.

PRAYER FOR THE DISARTICULATED

To all the bones that have lost their bodies—
may your ending be a whole one.

Osteoporosis is a petty beast,
may you never know its gnaw.
Rest whole my brothers and sisters.

May cancer's twisted song
never drift over you, you are
lost, but may you never turn cannibal.

The tooth fairy is a mother bear, she was only
meant to care for her children, the lost teeth,
but she has never been able to ignore an orphan.
If you hear the flutter of her wings, wail like all
lost children and she will sing you to sleep.

Oblivion is not your enemy. May it come
like the first dawning of spring, slow and peaceful.
When the bacteria and fungus eat you grain by grain,
do not worry about who you left behind. You are giving life
to a million creatures, the one you left behind will make do.
We miss you, I promise, there is a chorus of the boneless

singing your praise always. Our conductor has no
teeth and no fingers. To the complete he looks unmoving,
but to all who know the loss of our own body, he
crafts the most beautiful symphonies.

He tells us all to love what we had and not mourn what we lost.
I am the newest member of the choir, hear my song.
It is the dreariest of dirges, but I mourn not your passing
but my loss. I pray you forgive me.

MAP OF LONGING 5

Tonight, I am both historian and partygoer
in the Caverns of Longing, those empty
hollows that always echo.

Once, your teeth were the guardians of your
whole self, 32 fortresses made of bone, the
men and women who manned them were legends;
there was no greater station you could aspire to,
than Guardian of Bone, Flayer of Sustenance.

Nothing lasts forever, especially not heroes.
Five of the forts were broken by external threats.
The soldiers who guarded them became instant martyrs.
That's when the trouble began. The rest of the body
idolized the remaining teeth, spoiled them with feasts.

The guardians grew complacent, that most deadly
of sins, and slowly the castles hollowed out.
They laid empty, full of sludge and rotten sugar for lifetimes,
barely holding their shape until five young men, hollowed out
a canine, the sharpest one left.

The acoustics of hollowed-out bone are perfect.
They turned legend, failure, and decay
into a cathedral of noise. They played for no one
at first, all that mattered to them was noise,
and power-chord, and making sure that before
you died you didn't just say something, you screamed
it until you were hollow.

They played every night, the sounds of their frustration
echoing even in the toes, and slowly they came. Every
person inside the body who didn't know what they
wanted to say but knew they needed to say something.
Now all 26 remaining teeth are rambunctious places
of worship. A different kind of music playing constantly
in each one, to full crowds, a cacophony worth living for.

THE HEART OPENS FOR THE THOUSANDTH TIME

Remember, this is a museum,
not a library, we look, we love,
we reminisce, but we never remove.
Make sure you do not
disturb the spiders, they keep the place
free of pests. Don't forget
the air freshener, the smell of rot
is impossible to get out.
Leave the map at home,
this is a place for meandering.
Bring tributes, everything that
lives here sees itself as your Gd,
especially the dead.

SHE LIVES

Hope killed Reason and skinned
that bastard for warmth.

Hope counts the hawks every winter
and the snakes every spring.

Hope dances naked, dares you to even mouth
the word shame with every movement.

Hope has three teeth left
and smiles all the time, invites you to laugh.

Hope knows that she and poison both smell of almonds;
she loves the irony.

Hope dug a hole deep enough to bury us all,
threw away the shovel.

Hope has named every one of her scars,
her favorites are elegy, firelight, and Tennessee.

Hope loves skipping stones across the river,
always leaves a secret as payment, joy is never free.

Hope replaced her tongue with a flame,
knowing that we are all barely restrained infernos.

Hope knows that darkness has never been the enemy;
Hate always hides in the light.

Hope loves her sisters, Grief and Regret,
more than she loves breathing.

Hope is always the last one to leave family reunions,
Hope remembers everything worth remembering,

when she died/ everyone came to her funeral/ no one said a word./ As the line formed to dump dirt on her body/ Truth slowly walked past them all/ knelt before the body/ used her ring finger to peel her face off in one clean motion/ whispering something no one else heard, she did the same to her cousin's corpse/ swapped their faces./ The first thing everyone notices/ now are the stitches/ holding on Hope's face./ How Truth lies unmoving, lifeless, forgotten

OPTIMIST

I don't believe in luck,
but I still carry a two-dollar bill
wherever I go.

Which is to say:
I spend a lot of time
hoping I am wrong.

GENEALOGICAL HORTICULTURE

Family is a garden of bone and betrayal,
pride and promise, growth and growl.
Family is a prize-winning rose, petals
the almost black of deoxygenated blood.
Family grows slower than frozen molasses
and, if not cared for, wilts faster than a heartbeat.
Family thorns cut deeper than the surgeon's knife.

Clogged arteries and stubborn chins grow
on every family vine, each one thick as a grey beard.
Family cares not for season,
family will grow and survive
no matter how deep the snow,
no matter how hateful the sun.

Family is a choice. Family is adoption.
Family is those you trust no matter where
they first bloomed. Family is growth,
the intertwining of roots.

Family is knowing that often the most
inspiring flowers are transplants. Family
is a single Trinidadian Chaconia thriving
in our sea of stubborn nettles. Family is
a splash of brightest hope nestled in
our heart. Family is orchid, dogwood,
honeysuckle. Family is an impossible garden.

Family can be broken, the selfish axe
or the careless spark can burn what took
generations to cultivate.

Family is eternal. After every fire,
there are seeds on the ground.
Family is fertile soil. Plant only
what you wish the world to see.

MOURNING ROUTINE 82

When your grief is in full flood,
you must not be silent. Your
voice is the only anchor
you have to the people you
love, without it you will be
carried out to the center
of Lonely's sea. Truly lost.

Remember, you are not the
only one drowning. Your voice
will be the lighthouse that lets
them find the shore. Do not
let your fellow mourners lose sight of shore.

Today, clichés are your best friend.
Say them all— *My thoughts are with you,*
their memory lives on in you, it's
important to cry. Share your favorite
memories of the lost. What
you say matters far less than
giving your grief breath.

Don't worry about saying anything important,
clever is for people whose feet can touch the riverbed.
When you are in the middle of the floodwaters all that
matters is connection, they will only remember
the echoes of your voice.

Be quiet only when they are ready to talk,
take turns, throwing what hope and comfort
you can manage like the most important game
of Marco Polo you will ever play.
Only this time, none of you leave the water until
you have all been found, until you are all safe.

HEARTBEAT

I love the sound of my wife's
heartbeat. A metronome as permanent
as hope, as temporary as life

MY WIFE IS A SCHOOLTEACHER

I am too young for duck and cover.
I am too old for active shooter drills.
I am exactly the right age for students can
bring guns on campus during hunting season
as long as they are unloaded and the ammo's locked up.
I am exactly the right age for an angry ex-husband
shooting into the air in the parking lot because
his wife won't let him see his kid at the track meet.
I am the right age for Columbine, for this is an
isolated incident, for a friend to die in a massacre.
Three generations of fear and nothing has changed
except the makers of the fear sending their own
kids to safer schools in nicer shoes.

AN HONEST MOUTH

Sometimes I choke on the truth.
It writhes in my throat, a tiny
version of the man I want to be
struggling to climb, arms and legs
shattered by the fear
in my   body.

I know I could swallow him easily,
drown him in stomach acid,
never to be seen again.

To release him, I'd have to smash
both joints of my jaw
with a sledgehammer.

When you ruin everything with a lie,
you can apologize, try to earn back trust.
When you ruin something with the truth,
there is no way to fix it, nothing but
you standing there   with your jaw
bouncing against your chest,
a metronome of failure.

AN ARGUMENT FOR TRUTH

No one is going to tell you the
real reason you should not lie.

The pain you may cause is a good argument,
but to make it you must ignore the kindness
of the white lie. You must ignore that lies have the power
to improve the lives of those we love.

One may argue on the importance of truth.
Truth is the blood and marrow of a life well-lived,
but to make this argument you must ignore
that lies can teach us how to live better.

The existence of the tooth fairy teaches
us that everything has a cost.
Santa teaches us that joy is always possible,
even when the days are at their shortest.
"You can be anything you work for" teaches
us hope, the one thing life would not be
worth living without.

The real reason to lie as little as possible
is that we are how we spend our time.
If you spend it lying, then you are a lie.
It will become easier to lie every time you do it
and harder to know who you are. Soon, there will
be a stranger standing in your body, a forgery
living your life, a perjury pouring sickly sweet
fictions out of your mouth.

If you spend your time working to be better,
then you are better. Even when you fail. When
you spend your time hoping and working
towards your hope, then you are hope. Even
in the gutter, even sleeping behind a dumpster,
you will inspire. This is why we do not lie.

MOURNING ROUTINE 11

A prayer is anything that we do
that we give our entire focus to,
anything we focus on to the
exclusion of all else.

Every day, make the first thing you do for
someone else a prayer. Not to a faceless
Gd or to your grief, but to the moment.
It doesn't have to be a big thing.

Let someone else have the closer parking spot.
For that moment, think only that their feet will
ache a little less when they get home that day,
that they will get to hold their puppy
twenty seconds earlier because of you.

Make your wife's morning muffin perfect. Tune
out everything else in the world as you make
sure the butter is spread evenly, all the
way to the edge. Crack it just enough for
the heat to crisp the whole thing
but not enough for it to fall apart.

There will be things you have to do before you can muster
this kindness. Hate yourself for not dying first,
take twenty minutes to turn on the light, cry in the shower
cry again while getting dressed. Be reminded of the lost
by every breath. It's okay if this takes
most of your day. Grief makes us all a little selfish.

HAUNTED 2

Those who are afraid of ghosts
have never been haunted by the living.

My stepfather is dying in bed,
my mother stands over him saying nothing.

Only the dogs speak;
they never stop barking,

Death is walking through the kitchen,
and they are furious.

UNMAKING

We are all cannibals.
Knuckles are the popcorn of the human
body, crunchy but almost flavorless,
better with butter.

The eyes are tiny oranges,
sweet with a delightful pop.
I have lived 11 lives.

I haven't always become
a better person each time,
but I have always been
more.

I lived a life so full of rage,
each breath was furnace-hot and ragged,
leaving soot stains wherever I paused.

I lived a life where the only thing
I wanted more than
her touch was to believe in Gd.

I have lived three broken lives.
Once I broke myself.

Once betrayed
by a friend become brother,
and once broken
by others' pain
crusted into hate.

We cannot become someone
new until we not only see
our current self, but consume it.

You will have to unmake yourself
with tear and crunch,
one joint at a time, sinew by sinew.

Serve yourself one culinary
offering at a time. A rib here,
cooked low and slow, seasoned
with thyme and failure.

A finger there, twice fried and crisp,
coated in the hottest sauce you can stand.
The pain will be excruciating,
but if you don't rush it,
so will the joy.

This is something no one tells you.

ACKNOWLEDGEMENTS

This is a much more focused collection than my first book of poetry; it is focused almost entirely on the concept of grief and how we should approach it. I want to say in plain language that I know there is nothing in this world more personal and lonely than grief. There is also nothing I believe more wholeheartedly than the fact that, despite this, grief cannot be faced alone: you must find human connection to weather it.

The level of support I received while writing this book and going through the events that inspired it is truly something I could never have anticipated and that I find hard to believe I deserve. First off, I want to thank the unending and incredible support of my wife Tiffany Woodley and friends, Rico Frederick and Ben Baynton. I also want to thank my sister, Amanda Singer and my parents, Wendy Seay and Lewis Singer.

The incredible team at Button also made this book possible and supported me in every way I asked and a ton of ways I didn't know to ask. Thank you so much Tanesha Kozler, Charley Eatchel, and Izzy Miller. I also want to thank my wonderful cover designer Coral Black.

ABOUT THE AUTHOR

Jared Singer is an audio engineer and poet currently living with his amazing wife in New Jersey. He grew up in the Blue Ridge Mountains of Virginia and came to maturity in Brooklyn. This life has taught Jared that both beauty and hardship will find us wherever we go, and we cannot run from either. What we can do is choose which we look for and which we focus our life around. Jared is proud to focus his work on joy, science, and learning from his worst moments. This is his second collection of poetry, the first being *Forgive Yourself These Tiny Acts of Self-Destruction.*

AUTHOR BOOK RECOMMENDATIONS

***Afterwards* by Reagan Myers**

Too often when we discuss depression and beauty, we use the word *despite.* Reagan Myers knows better. With an honest flourish, she declares that she is both depressed and still magnificent, broken and still worthy, human and still honest. In her first collection, *Afterwards,* she explores, with a plainspoken but undeniable openness, the truth behind what it means to be ourselves. She teaches us that we are not objects created by our brains and our experiences, instead we are imperfect forges, capable of creating lives and legacies. This collection is not all darkness, Reagan laughs as well as she teaches, telling us what we need to survive anything our minds throw at us, reminding us to always have a "battery powered lamp and a therapist."

CREDITS

Assistant Editors
Charley Eatchel
Melanie Koopmans
Isabelle Miller
Sarah Tachau
Alix Wolf

Book Photography
Emily Van Cook

Cover and Interior Design
Coral Black
Charley Eatchel

Distribution
SCB Distributors

Ebook Production
Siva Ram Maganti

Editor
Tiffany Woodley

Publisher
Sam Van Cook

Publishing Operations Manager
TaneshaNicole Kozler

Publishing Operations Assistant
Charley Eatchel

Social Media and Marketing
Catherine Guden
Isabelle Miller
Eric Tu

OTHER BOOKS BY BUTTON POETRY

If you enjoyed this book, please consider checking out some of our others, below. Readers like you allow us to keep broadcasting and publishing. Thank you!

L.E. Bowman, *What I Learned From the Trees*
Patrick Roche, *A Socially Acceptable Breakdown*
Rachel Wiley, *Revenge Body*
Ebony Stewart, *BloodFresh*
Ebony Stewart, *Home.Girl.Hood.*
Kyle Tran Myhre, *Not A Lot of Reasons to Sing, but Enough*
Steven Willis, *A Peculiar People*
Topaz Winters, *So, Stranger*
Darius Simpson, *Never Catch Me*
Blythe Baird, *Sweet, Young, & Worried*
Siaara Freeman, *Urbanshee*
Robert Wood Lynn, *How to Maintain Eye Contact*
Junious 'Jay' Ward, *Composition*
Usman Hameedi, *Staying Right Here*
Sean Patrick Mulroy, *Hated for the Gods*
Sierra DeMulder, *Ephemera*
Taylor Mali, *Poetry By Chance*
Matt Coonan, *Toy Gun*
Matt Mason, *Rock Stars*
Miya Coleman, *Cottonmouth*
Ty Chapman, *Tartarus*
Lara Coley, *ex traction*
DeShara Suggs-Joe, *If My Flowers Bloom*
Ollie Schminkey, *Where I Dry the Flowers*
Edythe Rodriguez, *We, the Spirits*
Topaz Winters, *Portrait of My Body as a Crime I'm Still Committing*
Zach Goldberg, *I'd Rather Be Destroyed*
Eric Sirota, *The Rent Eats First*
Neil Hilborn, *About Time*
Josh Tvrdy, *Smut Psalm*
Phil SaintDenisSanchez, *before & after our bodies*
Ebony Stewart, *WASH*
L.E. Bowman, *Shapeshifter*
Najya Williams, *on a date with disappointment*
Jalen Eutsey, *Bubble Gum Stadium*
Meg Ford, *Wild/Hurt*

Available at buttonpoetry.com/shop and more!

BUTTON POETRY BEST SELLERS

FORTHCOMING BY BUTTON POETRY

Daniel Elias Galicia, *Still Desert*
Chelsea Guevara, *Cipota*
Mickie Kennedy, *Glandscapes*
FreeQuency, *(On |Un-)Becoming*
Hailey Tran, *an everyday occurrence*
Kristina Percy, *Both True*
Gigi Bella, *without the frills*
Adrienne Novy, *good luck in the real world*